waterway

T0353124

This One Is For You

releasing new voices, revealing new perspectives

This One Is For You

waterways
an imprint of flipped eye publishing
www.flippedeye.net

First Edition
Copyright © Agnes Meadows, 2008
Cover Image © iStockphoto.com/alfonso76
Cover Design © Petraski, flipped eye publishing, 2008

ISBN-10: 1-905233-19-1
ISBN-13: 978-1-905233-19-9

British Library Cataloguing in Publication Data
A catalogue record for this book is available from the British Library

Editorial work for this book was supported by the Arts Council of England

Printed and Bound in the United Kingdom

LOTTERY FUNDED

To Brinsley Sheridan,
poet, friend, and would-be blues superstar
I miss you, especially in Texas.

This One Is For You

Agnes Meadows
2008

This One Is For You

Contents

Mirror

I see you watching me.
I watch you seeing me.
Your eyes are insects, darting
Anxious and afraid.

Their uneasy reflections impale themselves
On my face, leave tiny pin-pricks of fright
Etched there, skitter away, fearful of
Capture, mute and driven.

A thin, joyless wedge of a smile colonizes
Your spider mouth, worries away
Nervously, barely settles, does not knit
Upwards into the grey nest of your iron eyes.

In daylight, empty of you, I move furniture
Back and forth in the room you call your own;
Your bed, the dresser covered in empty perfume bottles,
Coffee stains, dust, books exploring heat and madness,

Old shoes, your underwear, well worn, on the floor.
I wait for evening, the clock striking six, your key
In the lock, your deep sigh as you throw yourself
Across the room, catch me seeing you,

See me catching you. At night
I watch you sleeping, alone in your bed
Except for the reflections. Sometimes
You smile when you sleep.

Elements

You speak the language of the stones,
Hard, flinty words that
Roll and rattle over my heart,
Leaving bruises where they touch.

I speak the language of water,
Amorphous and persistent,
So that you become eroded,
Identity shabby and distorted.

Despite the flame of love, we speak
Different tongues, our dialogue muddied,
An unhappy collusion of elements resistant
To the possibility of alchemical change.

We turn from each other,
Thin-lipped and mute,
Recognising that all words
Are **not** created equal.

Rennes

An impatient wind, sultry as sex, resentful
And brooding blew us across the square
At Rennes, making his moss-green eyes fidget,
Rattling branches, time hardened leaves tossed
Like old dice under tables and into dusty corners.

In the darkness we watched
The eager flicker of bats,
Imagining pipistrel vernacular
As they veered fretfully away
From lamplight and cigarette smoke.

He gave me a gift of glow-worms
Harvested from a fence of brambles
And lavender, calling
My name softly from the shadows,
His voice awestruck with wonder.

And we laughed at the absurd poetry of years,
Of days without meter or punctuation,
Of wine like sunlight in the glass,
Became restless under a star-burdened sky,
Turned away from misery and tears,

Unprepared for the inter-stellar weight of solitude
That wove through constellations,
The rounded geometry of moons
Leaving us breathless and in love,
Lunar symmetry the touchstone of our adoration.

Locard's Principle of Exchange _

Half a year has passed since his leaving.
Now it is winter, and I hug myself like a child
Living alone under railway bridges,
Or on park benches where the trees,
Their summer leaves long shed,
Flick branches at the lifeless sky,
Rattling the unborn buds like breathing bones.

I staple myself together with regret and fury,
Trying to keep my internal heat intact.
Is this all there is? I ask the louring afternoon,
This work-worn wintry time,
My days fostered to indifferent kin
Who pass me like an unravelling package from hand to hand.
Is this all there is?"

Loneliness sinks feline teeth into my limbs,
And other lovers roll away from me,
Errant and fractured,
Like fragments of glass,
Each one leaving an obdurate scar,
Drawing blood in cherry ropes,
The fruit of love turned sour.

Yet I do not miss him;
Not his voice, his thoughts, his impatience,
Not his arrogance or lies, not his presence.
No, I do not miss him.
But I miss the thought of him,
Not the man he was, but the man I thought he was.

From the beginning our affair employed
Locard's Principle of Exchange,
A forensic notion suggesting that when two objects meet
An exchange takes place, each element altered
By what passes between them, and that in such passage
Death becomes an inevitable conclusion.

So it was with us,
For we bartered only what would grieve us most,
A mutual infliction of sorrow
That culminated in the mortality of feelings
Leaving us both wounded beyond repair,
A fatal exchange,
The homicide of love.

Total Eclipse

Your body in the darkness lies mutinously silent,
The distance between us now unbridgeable.
My heart finally acknowledges first contact,
That moment when eclipse commences.
Our life together suddenly obscured,
Our days of love a belt of bright points
Varying in size and separated by darkness,
Caught on the lunar limb
Like a string of Bailey's Beads.

The dimming is gradual,
A predictable process
In which we drift, rogue constellations
In a void of our own creation,
Passion's terminal decline.

When totality begins, we become glacial,
The temperature between us dropping sharply
So that every breath is tangible,
And birds go quiet, their instinctive perception
Finely tuned

To the irregularities of inconstant moons.

Five Poems From The Silk Road

Kyzyl Kum

Why would I need more than this cascade of stars?

The moon sabres a corridor of shadows,
Smiles her spectral smile, kisses the dust
As it billows skywards in ghostly plumes.
Cities become no more than mirages of clamour
In the surging, vibrant darkness,
Venus sequining that celestial blaze.
In the wine of evening I become intoxicated,
The desert murmuring gentle as owls.

Why would I need more than this?

Across The Kyzyl Kum

Trees frond the arrow-straight Kyzyl Kum highway,
Limp and exhausted in this unyielding air.
The tarnished road to Samarkand stretches relentlessly ahead,
Earth furrowed, overused and weary.

You ask too much of me, it sighs,
A careless lover paying me no compliments,
Scratching the surface of love
With your endless demands.

This desert stretches all the way to the lip of the world,
Plate flat, furze and scrub lending a random tear of yellow to the land,
Copper thorns jewelling rusted earth,
Pewter sand broken by heat and bitterness.

Sometimes rain pearls the golden road with its hoary coinage,
An occasional dream across the heart beat of the world,
Water, the silver thread binding nomad to horizon;
Air, a transparent mystery; faith, a dream within a dream.

Wedding At Shakrisabz

(Shakrisabz is the birthplace of Tamerlane, who ruled Central Asia in th.
14th Century)

Below Timur's scowling rough-hewn presence,
By his summer palace's monumental ruins,
The wedding party maintains convention,
Bride and groom anxious and unsmiling,
Her stone white face locked against happiness,
His eyes a gleaming pomegranate wound
Invading the inscrutability of nomads.

Around them a dignity of dusty friends
Spill like abandoned treasure across the statue's steps,
Moon-browed children shy with unfamiliar attention,
Dimpling coyly at the buzz of cameras,
Uncles and cousins rowdy with anticipated excess,
Grandmothers united in their diffident pumpkin roundness,
Grandfathers bleached of passion and ready for paradise.

We stand watching in polite yearning,
A group of drab foreign starlings
Caught up in the pleasure of the moment,
The golden toothed girls giggling and slender,
Their garments a garden of velvet and silk,
A dazzling floral brilliance set
Against the straggling municipal flowerbeds.

Then suddenly we are laughing together,
The bride giving a sly smile,
The groom rearranging his tie,
His unfamiliar suit collar,

While we kaleidoscope for photographs,
Angles and Uzbeks linking arms,
The fretful couple surrounded by grinning strangers,
Salaam Alaikum.
Walaikum Salaam.
May God give you grace
And a harvest of children,
The wide-faced boys showing more teeth,
The girls disappearing behind their hands.

And one day, in a week, or a year, or a lifetime,
Someone will look at those pictures
And remember that day when customs and cultures,
Miles and mother tongues,
Became an irrelevance
For a brief moment beneath Timur's statue,
Under an unbending sky.

On The Road to Samarkand

...we cross a land so barren
even a tree is cause for celebration,
where children wave from the roadside
and remember the waving for days,

where the horizon undulates
like a soft-breasted woman,
and only the birds leave shadows.

On the road to Samarkand we cross a land so bare
even a harvest of yellow thorn shrub
seems like a miracle,
where grass and brick and skin

are beaten into dun coloured uniformity,
sun-metalled and impregnable,
dervishes of dust snaking across the mud brown hills.

At Ulug Beg's Observatory

The plane trees turn golden at Ulug Beg's observatory,
Skylarks calling to the setting sun,
An orchestra of avian voices extolling life
In a joyful volley at the tomb of Timur's grandson.

Saffron leaves sift to the ground.
Roses, frayed by autumn's final breathing,
Cling to each other for comfort,
And the purple faded dahlia bow submissive heads.

The ladies of Samarkand beam their gilded pleasure,
Apple faces etched by the hands of history,
Coloured by the ghosts of forgotten ancestors.
And I find myself smiling at the thought of distant stars.

In Argyle Street

Past midnight.
He leans against a street lamp, alert to every possibility,
Eyes bleak with effort,

Boy, acid house-boy, emotions
Never to be freed from a silent mouth, shadows
Dancing on each corner, sombre as sorrow.

Time on the street, trading time,
Dawn too distant to think of as he leans, nervously
In the rain, the cars not stopping,

Broken eyes revealing a life gone stale
Between dusk and the rising of the moon.
He turns his face to the ashen sky,

Eyes closed, mouth a thumb-print bruise,
Skin no longer luminous, settling
His glance on those passing by without a smile.

Boy, past midnight cowboy, keeping the cold
At bay with memories blow-torching his body
To submission, promises broken so often
The knife-edge of hope is numbed forever in his heart

Alone in the pre-dawn hours, watching the minutes
Diluted in October rain, he dreams of a foxglove day
In autumn when he saw the leaves turn yellow,
He dreams of waking alone in a room filled with birdsong,

The flame of roses burning in the grate, white linen,
Unstained by the hours, tangled in the tangible silence,
The absence of hunger better than paid pleasure,
The key to his door hidden under his pillow...

He dreams.
He dreams.
He dreams.

Starbucks

The beggar comes in, toothless,
Face a dissolving map of indigo tattoos
Snaking across consumptive shoulders,
Down each well-tracked arm, his skin
The colour of pavements and gutters,
A crutch at his side to ease swollen feet,
Legs encased in grime-bejewelled jeans
For which water is a far off memory.

Spare some change, he rasps,
Voice grated raw by long nights spent in doorways,
By cheap rough cider and fag-ends retrieved from bus stops,
By years of dragon love and tin foil heaven.
Yet he has a strange, well-thumbed dignity.
He does not beg. He asks, quietly.
And it would be churlish to refuse him.

He buys a coffee, something hot
To keep the chill of solitude at bay.
And as he heads for the door, a child
Some six months old, bonny and brisk
In the safety of parental grip, looks up at him,
And smiles. He stops, a silvered gleam of homage
Touching eyes bleached by ancient longing.

They watch each other, beggar and baby,
For seconds, blue and brown eyes locking
In unspoken recognition, before each returns
To the life best known – to lap and to pavement.

Young Boy at a Poetry Workshop

Thin as a wheat-stalk broken after harvesting,
He walked through the door, shuffling and awkward,
Grown men's shoes clumsy on his young child's feet,
Toes gripping the leather lest, unclenched,
He might fall back into harder times.

His face was a locked room
In which the ghosts of Christmas past manifested,
Blue ragged curtain eyes drawn tight against the intruding gaze,
No shred of inner light escaping,
Not a dark look, just a blank one.

He spoke slowly in whispers,
His cracked gate voice banging against the frame of his throat,
Grating as if unused to speech,
As if denied the opportunity to manifest persona,
Internal volume stifled into silence.

A cynic might have thought that he had come solely for the biscuits
So complete was his focus upon them,
A concentration betraying unmerited lack,
Crumbs of comfort addressing
His most observable need.

But then he spoke of dragons,
And I knew he had been hooked
By more than hunger,
His a dual need; one visible, the other

Camouflaged by stoic emptiness.

Yet, I had seen his father with other, more
Satisfactory sons, well fed boys, their shoes
A perfect fit, snapping ordinary fingers,
Easy smiling eyes belying his chaotic ones,
Flame and scale subsiding into mute acceptance.

This cuckoo child, body angles sharp enough to wound,
Shoulders subsided into the blank highway of pre-pubescence,
Bled loneliness; a slow and stupid boy
Dismissed on sight by the prattling crowd surrounding him,
The pure poetry of his thoughts ignored as he spoke

Of dragons, his eyes lifting, unlocked
Prisoners taking their first steps towards originality,
Leaving the aspirant chatter behind as he alone soared skyward,
Voice a scale rasp of raptor's wings,
The beasts of his imagination tearing at the world.

Summer Vintage

She holds him like a room that she can enter to find herself,
A mirror in which her reflection can be seen again
Burnished to excellence, her face a symphony
Of jubilation, so brimming with joy any second she will lift
Skyward, even breathing becoming superfluous.

He touches her face as if she will disappear
Without his touch, storing the memory of her features in his fingertips,
Aware that time is running out, but not of the February wind that rattles
His bones, not of the buses that file wearily past, nor of the church
Clock chiming another quarter hour closer to departure.

And then they kiss, a private duet
Orchestrated for all to see, too elated to bother with discretion,
Passion's percussion compressed into that small space where lips meet
Lips – pure jazz, pure late-night syncopation –
Kiss,
Until they step back, dizzy in the eye of love.

To look at them you would think they are sixteen,
That they have never known love before, that this is the first
Time, so entangled, so unmindful, so glad of each other...
But they are both sixty if a day,
Savouring the very best of summer's vintage.

Calypso Woman

She calypsoed onto the bus
Ample and vibrant,
Lime-pickle sharp and pineapple bright,
Exuding life without circumspection,
Exaggerated and glorious,
Her presence a ringing, reverberating oil-can drum roll,
A tropical garden of ebullience
Her breasts a pitching Caribbean sea
That carried you forward into her luxuriant blackness
Like a boat beached on monumental landmasses,
Wrecked on the coral reef of her animation.

No-one could have said she was beautiful,
For she was the antithesis of magazine sleek or media chic,
Yet people couldn't take their eyes off her,
Her mango roundness delectable and fascinating,
Her laughter a full-blooded hyena cry that leapt from her throat
To tear the skin off any red riding hood wretchedness.

Marriage is a serious commitment, she crooned Jamaican-style
To two skinny-arsed friends pinned on her liquorice eyes,
Eclipsed by her carnival presence, her face alight with dreams
Of weddings and honeymoons, the love beyond reason
All women secretly desire, family waiting at the door for her
Weary return to re-establish safety. *You want to show everyone
You is Seeery-US*, emphasising the US with her sun-stroked lips,
A hibiscus wreath grin contradicting such solemn words.

And we knew he would have a happy life,
That impending husband yet to be captured,
And that every day he would marvel at his great good fortune.

Lifetime

(They had been married for over 60 years, the last 20 of which she had been suffering from Alzheimer's, while he had been her carer. When asked why he stayed, he said 'Because I love her.' This is for him.)

Come dance with me, my light-footed darling,
My heart, a river whose currents are hidden from sight,
Strong as the waking earth knows sunlight in April.
You are still lovely, my hearts-ease sweetheart,
And if you can no longer remember my name,
Do not fret, for I have enough memories for both of us.

Straight-backed I will lead you onto the dance-floor,
As proud of you now as in the beginning
When men more comely than I, and all their brothers, competed
For your hand. Spring was never far distant in those days of our courting,
Every day a ribbon of love that kissed the flowering sky with jubilant lips.
No day was brighter than the day that I claimed you,
No night as sweet as that in which you slept by my side.

It is more than my duty to watch over you. I do it for love,
My girl of the willow grace, your eyes the colour of beech leaves,
Faded now with the sun of too many summers.
I will hold you where you cannot stand and even familiar things become
                                                        unknown,
My name no more than a leaf swept away on the tide.

Today your face is soft as a child's
And I know you are far from me, walking
In the company of strangers whom once you held dear.

In that half-remembered realm you are alive again to the promises of
                                                        youth,
When every sky was star-bedecked and you could name your price
In the currency of adoration. They are all gone now,
Those laughing companions of primary seasons,

Each one lying at your feet like a lean boat,
Green and acquiescent as a hazel branch,
Impatient to carry you away.

Let them wait for a while longer, slender girl,
For I have need of you still.
And today is not a good day to be gone.

This One's For You

(For Brinsley Sheridan – 1940something to 2004)

This one's for you because I think the idea
Of it would make you smile, because, being Irish,
Words meant as much to you as song or family,
Sentences like wives bringing you comfort,
Life set against a harmonica blues backbeat
Unlocking the grief that occasionally rose to the surface
From the graveyard of aspiration that picketed your heart,
Made you play so raw it touched all of us,
Your notes cutting to the quick the way good music should,
Leaving us staring and exposed...

Because you wanted to be that blues man
Who left us ragged with longing,
Because you wanted to be that savage sex
God of rock for just a few minutes a week,
As an antidote to white middle-class smugness,
To tear the nails out of the complacent Stepford lives
Ambushing so many, to get the blood flowing, the heart pumping,
To bring life back to the suburban Nosferatu
For just a few wild minutes a week...

So this one's for you
Because a million love poems are written every day,
But not enough are written about friendship.

This one's for you to celebrate our connection,
And because I loved you,
Especially in Texas, when we rode together
Through the flood of April blue bonnets, dodging doggerel,
You fretting about losing your way, again, bemused
In a spider's web of freeways, Taco Bells, general stores
And late night bars...

Where you could strut your stuff with impunity,
Make the difference you had always wanted to make,
Again and again, because you were always,
Always better than you thought and your poetry kept me going
Sometimes in the dark night of *my* soul,
So this one's for you,
Because a million love poems are written every day,
But not enough are written about friendship.

This one's for you,
Because I wanted to write something without the tumult of fury,
A poem that talked about the way I loved you, quietly,
A book of silent hours written with the ink of stillness,
Resting with you like a smiling breath.
This love of the unspoken days;
a kiss on the mouth of brotherhood,
Because a million love poems are written every day,
But not enough are written about friendship
So this one's for you,
Yes, this one's for you.

Night Stain

Inspired by Michaelangelo's 'Study of Shoulders' – 1524

Ochre lines detail a tether of shoulders,
Dog 'Day' for the Medici Chapel,
A charcoal tribute of knotted limbs curved
Across the crumbling parchment
Signifying an obsession with form,
The endless passage of flesh
Pinpricked by moonlight and madness.
Night waits tight as an indrawn breath,
The sweat rising under his shirt,
Skin currented silently, restless
Anticipation beading his throat,
And a red wine blot illuminating one careless moment.

Entrapped by food and sin and loneliness,
The boy stirs, somnolent in gloom flicker,
Casts his vine-dark eyes across the room like a net.
They share a second of laughter, lips poised
For entanglement, before the charcoal coils again
In linear manifestation, glass-bound wine colouring
The candle's flame. He watches a plume of breath rising
And falling, the lash of shoulders taking shape
on another anticipating page, muscles gathering and binding
Under his hand, fingers stained with chalk and impatience.

The glass topples, a tower of desire.
One careless moment.

Red

Will Scarlet deep in the forest, locked
In Robin's embrace. Red-breasted Robin,
Glaring from the wintered holly bough.

Crimson berries joined in a jewelled wreath, pierced
By the eyes of Christmas. The ears of the fox,
Like flags, in a field of growing corn.

Scarlet fingered autumn burning fox-brush leaves
In mist-filled silence. Poppies, dancing
In their millions, remembering no wars.

Mahogany eyes of the Oak King, hair aflame,
Running across the heathered hill tops. Rosebuds garnered
In the rusted morning, no modesty amongst them.

Ruby mouth of the Beast, blood on his lips, covering you
With kisses; rage in his eyes, like flickering firelight,
He breaks you open in the wine-dark shadows.

Cranberry dawn stains the cheeks of the young
Girl blushing at midnight's remembered heat
And the hand of her lover on her naked breast.

Vines, drunk with power, hold the rosy grapes to ransom.
In the orchard, russet fruit dreams on the branch,
And the wild strawberry trembles in the ground.

Brazen copper sun, painted limbs awry, sleeps
Abandoned on a coral ocean. Fiery comet dragon
Lifts his garnet head and whispers, *I wait for the King.*

The Memory of Water

Silent now,
It holds the memory of stones,
Curling over their slate brown shoulders,
Smoothing away the pain of fragmentation with a curving touch,
Forging a pristine coiling path,
Mole-blind and shapeless,
Mute except when falling,
Restless with thoughts of roots and smiling Narcissus,
Leaping to be first at the dam.

Still now,
It remembers Friday nights by the hearthside,
Old tin baths unhooked from washroom doors,
And infants wriggling, slippery with soap,
Frills of foam ornamenting their tiny bellies,
Da breathing beer and sawdust,
And brothers and sisters bending under the weight of rainfall
As they run past coal thickened canals
Lacking even the ghosts of fish.

Smooth now,
It considers the tears of women
As they walk through bee-heavy heather,
Steepled together for comfort,
Keening for sorrow of love lost at sea,
Their grief reflecting the raucous *Why? Why? Why?* of herring gulls
Soaring above the relentless fidget of indigo swell,
Present in that small comma of attendance
Personifying pain.

Silent, Still, Smooth,
It peers from the kaleidoscopic bottoms
Of wells, trapped in moonlight,
Waiting for the body of winter.

Julia Pacata – Unhappy Wife, As to the Causes of Her Misery

From a fragment of Roman funerary wall circa 75AD, Museum of London: *"To the spirits of the departed and to Gaius Julius Alpinus Classicianus, Procurator of the Province of Britain,* **JULIA PACATA**, *daughter of Indus,* **his unhappy wife**, *had this built."*

Did she miss starlings and heavens encrusted
With recognisable constellations, moons pregnant
With summer, violet dusk blanketing daily noise, skies
Languid purple with the day? Did love
Lie like a white shadow on her heart,
And did she miss heat on her body?

Did she miss olive groves,
Where each tree was a son to her, whispering arboreal love
As she moved through their owl-grey trunks,
Crickets creaking in brisk cacophonous descant,
Sun like an apricot sweetening her skin?
Held fast within another English winter,

Its trees standing bald and naked beneath sleet's
Torn mantle, its hills snake-brown with bracken death,
Her fingers stretched blind and groping for an hour
Of warmth, no single friendly face to bring her comfort,
Did she long for familial laughter,
And did she miss heat on her body?

Did she miss the monumental minutiae of her life,
A tidal wave mosaic of petty pieces, each one
Prodding her with loneliness, reminding her
Of what she no longer possessed; that seam of
Unchanged hills alight with Tuscan lily-fire seen
Daily from her bedroom window, skies

Bright as peacock's tails unfolding; streets where
She knew each crack and crevice, even
The dust rising in familiar ringlets; where
Jokes were reciprocated carelessly, and the smell
Of food cooking left her weak with desire?
Did she miss new crushed wine and oranges, spices

From Africa, raisins and pomegranates ready in the dish,
Butterflies like plates flinging themselves in frenzy
Across the wild; red roses frowsy on the stem importuning
Any hand they touched; that sleep-scented security blanket
Of tribal closeness wrapped tight about her, every
Single part of it threadbare, every single day of it gone?

Or did she just miss heat on her body?

Juliet's Sister

I did not die for love. I lived despite it,
Each day a tomb in which the glory of his naked face rose
Like a beloved spectral sun, pin sharp and bristling with grief.

Memories torment me with their misery,
A tragic manuscript in which I was but a marginal
Note, insignificant and overlooked, whereas *she*
Blazed from each page like an impassioned torch
Overburdened with mystery and romance,
A resplendent star unlocked from her tower of filial duty
To ride with unicorns, embracing the cruel enigma
Of love unconditionally, ready for sacrifice,
Crucified by it, yet lovely, still, as any
Poet's lasting accolade, so that the heart constricted
Imagining those radiant eyes closed forever.

She *was* the sun, brilliant and shining, forever
At zenith strength. And he, weak and foolish Montague,
Was bedazzled by her luminosity, so that, stepping back
Into the unlit chamber of my presence, he became blind
And unseeing. *I* was the moon to him, eclipsed,
Ignored, invisible, hidden beneath the layered
Clouds of faery glamour her presence guaranteed.

He did not even know my name, yet
My eyes were just as blue, not as sapphires
Stolen from the heavens and given life within her face,
Rather as lakes at midnight, too dark to be fathomable.
My lips paid tribute to no rose, my breasts no fragrant garden
Where love could be screened, my body no resting place,
No dream within a dream. He was a boy who loved not wisely

But too well, I a mirror to his folly, unnoticed and intangible.

Time passes. I take a step closer
To oblivion, eternity's fulfilment close at hand,
Indulge in imagination, basking in its fleeting warmth,
My self-made memories replacing truth. I see them
Growing old together, she become fat and impatient
With his boyishness, he wearied of that impatience, finally
Seeing beyond the beauty and the legend, tired of passion,
Turning away from the madness of obsession, seeing me
At last across another crowded room, smiling
That aching smile. My heart fumbles in my breast,
A flock of birds ready to burst free;
I step forward into the light.

Grania's Lament

For her husband Finn MacCumhail and her lover Diarmuid ua Duibhne.

I could not love him
          though his eye was dark
          as mountains with a storm upon them,
          his mouth a poem that had never been
          snared by the impatient pen,
          his body a bridge between two worlds,
          a skylark fletching the flax-flower heavens,
          unreasonable with wonder.

I could not love him
          though he was the hero of
          a thousand battles,
          his hand a net that had captured
          the hearts of men and held them
          fast like an army, breathless,
          in that moment of silence before
          the commencement of conflict.

I could not love him
          though he had hooked the Salmon
          of Knowledge, tasted the tempest
          of power in the flesh
          of the fish, its silver scales
          blinking and rippling, its breath a froth
          of inspiration, a shout of
          triumph as it bit into death.

I could not love him
          though his heart was a song
          gifted by blind harpers, beloved
          of the Ever Young as they rode out

on Beltane Eve, dressed all in
scarlet and gold, a hawk on each wrist,
and a web of emeralds and
pearls on each throat.

I could not love him
though his love for me
was a stag in spring,
a roebuck
leaping from crag to crag,
a deer stepping lightly,
dizzy with longing through
bee-beguiled heather.

I could not love him
because I had seen
Diarmuid. On the night of my wedding,
with the marriage feast spread out before
me like a carpet of joy, the echo of my vows
still sibilating in the rafters, the pipers holding
the moon to ransom, I had seen

Diarmuid,
and in that instant of seeing I
had become husbandless, ruined
by the lightning thrust of magical
intrusion, Diarmuid's glance
a sword, a shipwreck, a plague,
bringing with it only grief
and dishonour.

And time had fallen away from me
as I fled into the night

carrying nought but my shame
and the faery curse that blighted us both,
his glance like a lake in the morning
with the sun on it, and the Love Spot
the cause of all our sorrow.

Kernow Cariad

My love brings me stones,
Salt-rheumed and tide-lashed,
Bruised by mermaids,
Myrghes ap dowrow, daughters of water,
And carrying the memories of seal-song.

My love brings me orchards,
Heather purple-plaiding clifftops,
Blackberries from the roadside,
Enys Avallow, island of apples,
And the dark curl of adders whispering underground.

My love brings me tin,
A treasury of wheels a-gleam at Geevor and Botallack,
They spinning corridors of power deep undersea,
Map ap amserow, the sons of time,
History's grey coinage slipping through the hands of men.

My love brings me ravens,
Shadow black their oil bright wings,
Wild children of the Morrigan,
Myghternes breselow, Queen of Battles,
And a tempest of gulls tearing the wind with their weeping.

My love brings me children,
Brine-hearted, each one a wave
Light-stepping to shore with their white foam feet,
Myl folennow lyfrow, book of a thousand pages,
Their limbs the mottled pewter gleam of shoaling mackerel.

My love brings me wells,
Fair Lady of Madron bedecked in hawthorn berry,
Skirted in nettles and briar strewn,
Gwrageth gwyn keow, bridge of white hedges,
Her hair a tree of promises.

My love brings me harbours,
The dancing curtsey of bright dressed boats,
Eternal weave of prow and stern,
Splan gweder myras myttynow, bright mirror of morning,
The catch of fisher folk safeguarded from hurricanes.

My love brings me legends,
Of kings gathered at Lanyon on the day before end-time,
Swords aloft, their waiting knights each armoured in silver,
Gwer haf gwlasow, green country of summer,
And maidens so comely, their eyes a grief, their hands a heartbreak.

Smoked Sparrows

When I was a child
I could wake to a carpet of sparrows,
Their bracken-feathered wings
A rustling, fidgeting forest,
Bitumen eyes seed-pearl bright,
Their ubiquitous presence an un-notated symphony
On the telegraphic high wire.

They would pool on branches,
Jostle for crumbs at the pavement's edge,
Tamed by plenty,
Unafraid and swaggering,
So prolific you could not count them.

This spring a man told me
That in a shop in Barnsley he had seen
Tins of smoked sparrows on skewers
Brought all the way from China,
A gastronomic delicacy at £5 a tin.

I imagined them spitted in their tiny Oriental coffins,
Hearts bamboo-pierced and featherless,
Their claws folded into permanent oily curls,
Shoulders echoing the curved hunch of tin can corners,
Eyes and beaks glued forever shut,
Songs forever silenced.

Gone from London's streets a decade or more,
They are avian exiles alien as lyre birds or budgerigars,
Their absence an unsolved Cockney mystery,

East End children ignorant of the pleasing touch
Of sparrow's feet on outstretched palms
On Sunday's park-filled afternoons,
Their strident, brassy chirrup announcing presence at ankle height.

Any day now I anticipate
The McSparrow (with fries on the side).

Boxer Rebellion

This afternoon the beach bristles with weekend folk
Making a holiday of scant December warmth for an hour or so.
Mist soft serpent coils across the water,
Dulling surf's rushing whisper as it scrambles to shore,
And sky and sand both hold the sharded memory of sunlight –
Thin and fragile as glass.

A woman walks two Boxer pups onto the strand.
They pull and drag on the leash straining to confront
A growling, muscular sea,
Wind-swept and impatient to be off,
Wait, she burrs, voice taut with love and pride,
Wait my lovely, wait my 'ansome,
Wait...wait... wait.

They wait, legs splayed into the sand,
Noses pebble-dashed with the tiny grains of beach flotsam,
Tail stubs a-ticking like manic clock-work fingers,
Rumps quivering with anticipation,
They wait, panting and coiled with excitement,
They wait...wait...wait....

Until unleashed at last,
Two canine arrows darting to the water's edge,
Tongues flagging the air,
Legs pistoning paw for paw at equal gait,
Wheeling and swerving in tandem as if remote controlled from afar,
Tumbling into the surf together,
Punching foam and spume with eager paws.

But that wintry sea had long forgotten warmth,
Covering their muzzles with glacial kisses that
Had them yelping in icicled surprise, slipping
And lurching away from such arctic love,
Breath frozen in instant shock,
The water's raw bite halting even their adolescent zeal,
Abrogating freedom,
So that they bounced back, tails between their legs,
Back to their mistress,
All chase refrigerated out of them,
Knocked out in round one by the prize-fighting ocean.

Some Boxers they turned out to be!

Attic

In the attic,
Shrouded with ribbons,
Pale and blind,
Letters from old lovers die in boxes.

They whisper under the rafters,
An abandoned colony of words
Rendered impotent with age
Tolling desire's last resonance.

Air waits like a stopped clock
Un-breathed and redolent with dust motes.
Silence crouches grey as dusk-bred cats
Wreathing the year-darkened pages.

The Study of Clouds

Nephology – the study of clouds.
Entomology – the study of insects.
Dendrology – the study of trees and other woodland plants.

...the study of transforming seasons.
...the study of the healing heart.
...the study of the hopeful day.

He touched my face and called me beautiful,
Smiled his small, tired smile,
And I felt myself thaw from the burgeoning frost of middle-aged indifference,
Acknowledge the study of that single breaking moment
When all things had become a living possibility again,

The recognition of molecular change in my blood's capacity
For abundance, a continental shift of consciousness away
From treachery, a spectral exorcism,
The ghost of his mouth chiming on mine like a midnight clock.

He led me into the probability of expectation once more,
The dance of his body's percussion descanting direction,
He touched my face, called me
Beautiful,

...the study of the unlocked gateway.
...the study of the reclaimed kingdom,
...the study of the acquiescing spirit,

Philology – the study of the beloved word
Cartology – the study of maps and changing dynasties
Astrology – the study of star logic.

Alchemy – the study of transformation.

View from a Moving Train 2

Rain feathers Lindisfarne,
Heavens bleak as an Abbot's heart.
Gulls frill the wave-shaved cliff face,
While surf replicates itself in perfect, gloomy rolls.

Every tree and shrub lists perilously,
Drunk with wind, branches pulled thin,
Buds gasping in sleet-streaked Easterlies.
And then, of a sudden, fingers of sun prod the waves awake,

Blister its grey, seething surface with a million
Blind, white pods of foam, set the time-stroked
Leas afire, fast-forwarding from stalky glumness
To wheat-stem yellow grins in seconds.

Seasons change a dozen times this hour;
One moment skies clear as sapphires,
The next pregnant with indigo clouds
Stacking up on Northumbria's louring horizon.

Holy Island waits, a distant clinging snail upon
The walls of grey-green surf, drowning in Evensong
Bells, the gospelling mumble of monks at worship,
Their words navigating pages clean as sails.

The Lhiannan-Sidhe

Her beauty a danger, a prison, an iron cage,
A ruthless seduction, a negation of hope,
A destruction of charity.

So beautiful, men faltered mid-step
Their dusk-blighted homecoming forgotten,
Wives and kin unstitched in their minds,
Children turned to wraiths on the hearthstone,
Their prayers a catechism of doom.

So beautiful, men lost their sight in the seeing of her,
Stumbling forward into the green rippling field of her,
Trees hiding their shadows for shame of the light of her,
Her hair flowing undimmed, threaded with cowslips and clover,
A waterfall in winter, the hair of her.

So beautiful, men fell in the May woods at sight of her,
Kissed the earth as if seeking the mouth of her,
The bluebell mist rising up to cover them
Rendering them invisible, woven into the ground,
Bodies weakened with wanting, their bones spelling the name of her.

And she, turning away,
Forgot them more swiftly than footsteps,
Deaf to their loss-filled keening, a wound in the twilight.

Penwith Afternoon

There's something about the light on the water,
Ripples warmed by the sun,
Reflected sky a mirror of tangible balance,
That defuses the blister of anguish grid-locking my heart,
offers the sanctuary of contentment.

The water smiles with me,
Sea sprawling its heathen Cornish strumpet beauty,
Its surface fidgeting with sunlight across Mounts Bay
All the way from Marazion.
And I laugh aloud,
I laugh aloud, because I can.

Outside **The Dolphin Inn** trawler men
Slouch, their legs akimbo, redundant in the yawning
Afternoon, their faces marbled as shore-side stones,
Around them a cacophony of boats
Magnetised to the harbour.

At Newlyn I watch a seal sleeking the surface,
Head periscoped out of the forest-dark water.
It circles empty lobster pots,
Cuts through the winking embroidery of fish scales,
Teases herring gulls to frenzied, shrieking fury.

Sitting in that Penwith afternoon, watching
The light's somnolent topple into dusk,
Waves stretching lazy, sleep-beguiled, fingers,
Eternity looses its sting, becomes, not a thing
To fear, not a terror, but a languid possibility,
A moment of grace.

Sennen in December

Sennen in December. Wind whisks
Across the Atlantic, past Land's End
And Longships Lighthouse, over heather-clad
Cliff tops a-ghost with frost,
Bowling and blustering, fingernails
Of foam scratching and scouring the sea's surface,
The promise of snow scowling in the air.

People turn inland, shoulders hunched, hands
And noses anaesthetised, their breath
Snatched from their lips as soon as it is breathed.
Warmth and comfort only dimly remembered,
Summer a myth, remote and unattainable.

In the **Old Success** (established 1691) fire
Curls in the grate, an island of cheer, providing
Sanctuary and ease, spray-smeared windows
Filtering winter out. This Inn is filled
With wrecker tales, the souls of Cornish pirates,
Grim and over-cutlassed, a-slumber in its bricks,
Walls thick with legends and age-stippled

Pictures of ancient ships lying broken
On the jagged rocks, their cargos spilled and vulnerable,
Rum from Jamaica no longer recognisable.
Smoke finger-prints a ceiling slung so low
Grown men rise slowly from their seats,
Heads bowed in anticipation of damage,

Hands roughened with the herring haul,
Cupping pints of the Black Stuff as if it was precious.
They talk of tides and tempests,
Waves rising like an army of walls
Replicating endlessly, each one requiring
Concentrated domination.

In secret they are afraid,
For they know they can never win.

Photograph

"A boy walks past a bullet ridden wall as he enjoys a lollipop in Kabul."
(Nov. 12.2007 – MSN News)

That this boy could still have mischief in his eyes,
Could still grin like a door wide open,
Could still be easy in his shoes.

That this boy could still taste the ghost
Of strawberries in cheap sweets,
Still savour the sugaring stab of them on his tongue,
Could still imagine himself blessed at such a gift.

That this boy could still look
With wonder at an empty sky,
Watch skeining birds net November clouds,
Follow a heron on the wing.

That this boy could still say hello to strangers,
Could still trust learning,
Remember the pleasure of kites,
Imagine the fathering of children.

That this boy could walk uncaring past a wall
Confettied by shrapnel, the gouging lace of bullets
Knitted into the ground, be blind to the unravelling
Tapestry of craters seaming his pathway home.

That we could still turn away –
Indifferent – forget him in an instant,
Could still just turn the page.

Thank you for buying *This One Is For You*. It is Agnes Meadows' third poetry collection with us. The others are *Woman* and *At Damascus Gate on Good Friday*. You can find out more about her at: http://loose-muse.com/agnes-meadows/ and follow her on twitter at: @AgnesMeadows1

—§—

the waterways series is an imprint of flipped eye publishing, a small publisher dedicated to publishing powerful new voices in affordable volumes. Founded in 2001, we have won awards and international recognition through our focus on publishing fiction and poetry that is clear and true, rather than exhibitionist.

If you would like more information about flipped eye publishing, please join our mailing list online at **www.flippedeye.net**.

Lightning Source UK Ltd.
Milton Keynes UK
UKHW010721210321
380690UK00002B/95